Also by Bummi Niyonu Anderson

I Like it When: A Collection of Love Poems

You are a Masterpiece: Seeing Yourself as God Sees You

Gumbo Soul: Book of Poetry

Moods:
Haiku and Other
Poems

MOODS:
HAIKU AND OTHER
POEMS

Bummi Niyonu Anderson

Chapter headings taken from "Moody's Mood for Love."
Lyrics by Eddie Jefferson

ISBN-13: 978-0578490144

ISBN-10: 0578490145

Editing: Mary Gervin
Cover Design: Femi Anderson

For
Dr. Asylvia Smith (2018)
Ms. Rosemarie Mundy-Shephard (2016)
Mr. David Young (2018)

RIP my college professors.

As a writer, what I learned from each of you is immeasurable. My life has been enriched because our paths crossed.

To Godmother Mtamanika
Thank you for giving me a place to rest my mind
and to create much of what is contained here.
And for giving me space to live free.

From the Poet

I started writing this collection of poetry four years ago. As a writer, I never know what will become of what I write. I never set out to publish. I only set out to write with the hope that others can identify with what I've written.

Moods: Haiku and Other Poems is about the multiplicity of moods or emotions we experience in life. Starting in 2015, I dealt with a gamut of emotions— rejection, love, loneliness, happiness, depression, uncertainty, fear, and freedom. Yes, freedom. Freedom is not only a thing or an ideal. It is a state of mind.

I hope you enjoy this collection of poems....

-Bummi

CONTENTS

II.   Shine Above

I.

You give me a smile and I'm wrapped up in your magic...

A Funny Thing Happened

I didn't see you the first time I saw you,
But I remember the moment I did.
My mind returned from a thousand miles at the
sound of your laughter.
My thoughts suddenly joined the rest of me;
I wondered where you came from
And how I could get there.

I watched your lips form every single word;
Your accent made me think crazy thoughts.
I should have been eating,
But I stopped to watch you.
I wondered where you came from
And how I could get there.

I wanted to ask you many questions,
Most of which to hear you speak your mind:
What do you do when it rains?
Are you afraid of anything?
Is there a dream that still inspires you?
My heart desires to know yours
And maybe just maybe,
You'd tell me where you come from
and
how I can get there.

I

Always radiant;
Kinetic with graceful flow;
Uniquely shining.

I Sat Across from You

I said I would not stare
When you sat down across from me.
I kept my word to myself but I wanted to.
Instead I listened to you;
Found out what makes you who you are.
I watched you smile at funny things
And smirk at my crazy insistence.
Your smile makes my heart melt like ice in the
sun;
I forget whatever has me troubled.
Today, I got an irreplaceable gift
One that cannot be measured or appraised.
My gift sat across from me.

2

My head said goodbye
Then I gazed upon your face.
Love beckoned once more.

3

Aimlessly looking;
Hopelessly dreaming of you
Is wishful thinking.

I Can Always Dream

Go away!
At least that's what I tell myself.
Until I close my eyes
And you're there
In my dreams.
I can touch you
And run my fingers
              through your coiled
                        Salt and pepper hair.
I kiss you and
          you kiss me.

Your body is like a winding road,
And I get to enjoy every curve
              of your chocolate skin.
              My lips taste every inch of you;
              I can't get enough.

Go away!
When I close my eyes
I dream of you
              again.
              Again
              And again.

Aretha

The Queen of Soul died yesterday.
A Thursday.

A piece of me left
And remained away...

Her voice jolts through my body
Like an electrical current.
Shocked me back into a new reality—
Love hurts like hell,
But...
        Wins
        Hates
        Teaches
I went searching.
No one was home.

Endearing and soulful—
I hear her singing in the quiet of the night.
Melodies dance
Sounds permeate me.

I look for soul—
Life twisted with joy and pain
With golden sunshine and pelted rain.

Aretha.

For another day.

4

You opened my mind
And read each page of my dreams
Like thoughts are dancing

Nerves

I want to talk to you,
But my voice goes silent.
I want to spend a moment with you,
But my fears grow stronger,
Stopping me from taking a leap
Into the unknown.

Invite me to come & sit at your table.
Help me overcome my fear of you.
Take a chance.
Chances are as moments;
Coming and going without warning.
I don't want to miss you;
But I just haven't mustered the nerve
To take a chance.

5

The love of my life
Is also the source of pain.
My fear cannot hide.

Unguarded Heart

If I had known you'd steal my heart,
Maybe I could have prepared for it.
But it would have been a waste of time.

I didn't see you coming,
Even as close as you were already
I was taken off guard.
Taken aback by your radiant smile,
It knocked me off my feet:
Made me think of nothing else.
I realized sunshine comes in many facets.
Your honeyed words tantalized me;
Made me think I want more of you.
You listened to me
In moments of distress.
You calmed every part of my being.
My mind no longer raged like angry waters.

Saturday Morning Dream

You made your way into my quiet space.
No not today!
I can't think about you,
I choose to love you from a distance.

I'm tired from not having you near
And wishing for what will never be,
Only to be distracted until Monday morning.
All because I let you into
My Saturday morning dream.

When A Poem is Born on Wednesday

I was awakened by thoughts of you.
My dreams flooded by your presence
And enchanted by your smile.
You make me want to see you,
If only for a single glance.

I stare into space
Wanting to hear your voice,
Wondering if you are thinking of me.
I close my eyes to go back to sleep
You return to my dreams.
My eyes follow you,
Mesmerized by your quiet smile.
I want to talk to you,
I'll tell you I'd never purposely hurt you,
Listen to the thoughts of your heartfelt thoughts.
I'll love you and then love you again.

Morning sounds waken me,
But I refuse to open my eyes.
I want to spend as much time dreaming of you as I
can,
If I open my eyes our tryst will end.

I go back to sleep and find my love waiting
In the corner of my mind.

6

I have kept your name
Locked away in my heart's room
Never to escape.

As an Orchid

Your smile is as dazzling stars

And always radiant like the sun,

As magical as the moonlight off calm ocean
waters,

You are beautiful.

Your heart always open to love

And to listen.

No matter the craziness of my thoughts,

You bring sanity to my earth,

With you I can do anything.

You are amazing.

Like an orchid,

Your beauty is rare.

Perfection personified.

7

Chocolate kisses.
A sense of moonlight misses
Before the sunrise.

Old School Soul

I gaze upon you. And I wonder
wonder
      wonder
Who's loving you.

The thought of ideas connecting is kismet.
The moment I wake up
I say
A little
      Prayer for you.

Sit down next to me.
The sound of the rain reminds me
nothing good
comes
      easy.
I wait for your love.
Show me a river that's so deep.
Show me a mountain so high.
Love is the air
I breathe.

Breathe in. Breathe out.
         Breathe in. Breathe out.
         The doctor says I'm congested.
            I inhaled too much of you.
Breathtaking...
Intoxicating...

Searching

I'll search until I find you.
Your being drives me.
You are treasured as diamonds and gold.
And when I find you,
I'd hold you close to me,
Listen to your heart
Let you tell me your dreams and your fears.
Finding you would finally fill my empty heart
I opened just for you.
The world may as well be flat
And time can just stand still.
Until I find you I've
Singled among billions
And the search is worth more than millions.

8

I call out your name.
I want to say so much more.
Words befuddle me.

As the Sun Sets

The sun is always setting somewhere;
Seemingly settling in for a nighttime snooze
But somewhere in the midst of my dreams,
Thoughts of you never, ever slumber.
The sun and moon share space in my universe.
Stars sprinkle both night & daytime skies.
My earth revolves around the sun and moon,
It's cosmic and unreal all at the same time.
Time never ends.

A Dream Come True

What am I supposed to do with a dream that is
you?
Pretend you didn't happen
Or try never awake?
I don't want thoughts of you to desert me
Though I know thoughts change.
When I need a smile and can't find my own,
I think of yours.
It reminds me of what is right in the world,
Even if my day is in chaos.
Some mornings I wake up after you've been in my
dreams.
I beam with joy at the memory of you.
It seems so real.

9

I have strong feelings,
But I hide my love for you.
Hoping you'll find me.

10

Being my true love,
As the eyes of the world gaze
I see only you.

Talkin' Trash: Love & BBall

The ball is tipped at half court.
I lose the tip and
Start defense.

First Quarter:
      I watch you.
      People love you
      And they gravitate toward you
      I get lost in the crowd.

Second Quarter:
      I love you.
      I gravitate towards you.
      I get lost in you.

Third Quarter:
      Sweet, but I can't.
      You might hurt me
      I can't deal with that.

Fourth Quarter:
      I can make no commitment
      I'll not hurt you
      I can promise you
      I'll never intentionally hurt you.

      Kiss me.

Swish

Game winner

The sweet sound of victory...

II

I love your image
Staring back at me sexy
Beautiful brown eyes.

II.
Bright as stars that shine
above you...

12

God hears in silence
Sees me in pitch black darkness
I can never hide.

13

Waiting for Him still,
Mounting with wings like the eagle
Preparing to soar

Ali: The Greatest

When a gladiator falls,
some celebrate his demise.
They stand on the giant
with raised fists of victory.
Goliath is down.

However ferocious the fists,
you were not a brute.
You were the people's champ,
And the people loved you.

When you fell,
we knelt down and loved you.

14

Strong men know themselves
An intense fire burns inside
To ignite others.

102 Howell
(For George Howell and Mtamanika)

I come to you bound,
Breaking from my own prisons
Freedom safety.

I sat on your porch.
I know you were there with me
As I sat listening.

The sound of your voice
My heart becomes ocean wide
Where Godmom's love flows.

15

I will tell no one,
But my entire being knows
I cannot hide from me.

16

Mistakes are teachers.
Learn what you can and test well
Start lessons again.

My Beautiful Black People

My beautiful black people
Come in all shades and sizes.

My beautiful black people,
You're like coffee without cream:
Strong, dark, and rich.

My beautiful black people,
I look upon you with an uninhibited gaze.
Colorful.
Powerful.
Awesome.

Hail to Nina!

Beautiful
Black!
Bold!
Soul Sistah!
Mother of the Movement!

Nina Simone is a freak of nature!
Your voice
A force like a hurricane
Booming down like driving rain;
Pelting truth against American walls of racism.
Every word as lightning, electric striking with
ferocity.
Lyrics powerful like the wind
While every man waits for the wind to calm,

Beautiful!
Black!
Bold!
Soul Sistah!
Mother of the Movement!

Mama Nina, your voice is as rushing, powerful
water.
Songs flood my mind with revolution:
You sang, "Everybody knows about Mississippi
Goddam!"

But, America... Goddam!
What have you done?
Are you angry enough yet?
How many of the black & the brown have to die?
Do you even care?

Nina Simone asks.
I ask.
Do you even care?!
Do you even care?!

Beautiful!
Bold!
Black!
Soul Sistah!
We are the children of Nina Simone!

We The People

A People...
As beautiful as any sunrise,
Stretching across the Atlantic,
Chained together across the waters
By the lineage of Africa.

A People...
Having our own language and culture,
Unknown to those who captured us
And taken to a land not uniquely ours.
We cultivated the very soil on which we stand.

A People...
Often beaten and bruised,
Lynched and scarred,
Sold and separated,
But wouldn't be broken in spirit.

A People...
Standing when kneeling,
But never bending to the wretched.
Hopeful in the storms of raging seas
That sought to make us casualties.

A People...
Whose writers write with pangs of admiration
Though the pen may drip with tones of pain.
Painters brush strokes of ambiguity,
The colors of our stories bold.

We birth life in the dance.

We the People...
African, yes African!
American, yes American!
Human, yes human!
Citizens of the world
                    We. Citizens of the world!

And the world knows us,
Sees us.

We the People.

17

Gracefully aging,
You are as fine wine preserved
And always treasured.

Humanity

Who is alien?
The dangerous
Those who hate just because
The sun came up in New York
And set in Bangkok.

Where are the humans?
Enjoying life,
Finding common bonds,
Loving those they want,
Grieving the loss of a total stranger.

Who are the haters?
Bitching about what is wrong with the world
But destroying rather than changing and
Tripping over the menial
As If the world should stop to say hello.

The earth is moving but
Not always dancing.

What is love?
Love is not always agreeable,
But has listening ears.
Love is not beautifully perfect,
Yet is open to alternate imperfections.

Humanity is as a mirror...

                    Always reflective.

18

Retire with sixty;
Drop the mic with "Mamba out."
Standing ovation.

Aunties

Aunties—
Be like mamas and they be fly.
These sistahs be
Fun,
Sassy,
Sly.

Auntie—
Is beautiful just like her sister
And a brother knows
He can't dismiss her.

For Rosemarie

Roses are beautiful in a bouquet;
All nestled together in a vase.
But just one rose is so exquisite:
One rose says hello, I love you,
And extends itself alone,
Its beauty beheld.

You were a special rose.
We smiled in your presence.
Your luster never faded
As you gave to us
And shared with us,
One blossoming Rose.
Always in season,
And blooming still.

19

When I close my eyes,
Your presence overwhelms me.
Reality check.

Reinvention

I
am finding
myself through you.
You liberate my mind;
my walls now have spaces
As the bricks are being removed.
Becoming like a woman at Brewster's Place
With my hammer, chisel, and whatever works
fine.
Or talking my way out of my own prison
You make me see I am freely holding the key.
The sunlight is not as shielded as it once was--
dark;
I can see it radiating, beaming,
Dazzling like a ballerina dancing.

I do not have to pretend with you,
I can be true:
Express my heart with no shame.
You ask me questions no one else dares.
Suddenly I find myself exploring what you
inquired of me.

Time with you is evanescent.
Introspective ramblings.
Moments remind me life is living.
What is life if wasting?
You hope for happiness;
Dream for me
To be,
Finally.

Albany

You reared me
From a shrub into a powerful tree
With my own branches stretching wide.

And I love you.

A city strong and unbending
And not wavered by strong winds nor driving
rain.
Albany is as a tree, planted.

And I sit under you.

Albany is the Good Life City
Planted by fluctuating waters.
I know your imperfections yet I see your beauty

And I stand with you.

20

Time warps into age.
When I no longer climb trees
I watch time march on.

Black Bodies
*(Inspired by Nina Simone/*Her Rendition of *Strange Fruit)*

Black bodies lying on the asphalt of American streets.

Police standing with raised guns at their feet.

Blood flows from black bodies as a stream

Into the painstaking sounds of a mother's scream.

A black man was murdered yesterday and left to die

His father beat his fists against the wall, asking why.

A black boy was walking home and followed by a crazed man.

Shot in cold blood so we put on hoodies to take a stand,

But Lady Justice failed once again;

She blindly turned away with no remorse or disdain.

Black bodies standing on an American sidewalk,

Approached by policemen with very little talk.

Why have black bodies being taken into custody become a death walk?

Sandra Bland, I will call her by her name.

Her black body left to die in a jail cell has brought her fame.

Black bodies no longer hang from sturdy trees,

But left to die on the asphalt of American blood-drenched streets.

21

Nubian woman
Beautiful as the sunset
Awe inspiring sight.

22

When friends are present,
I stand on top of the world.
Life made bearable.

Mother's Love

A mother's love is as vast as the ocean
With selfless care and unwavering devotion
With no lines to define
Or boundaries to confine
Endless and overflowing.

Dangerous

Denial is the best course of action.
Plead the fifth.
Wait.
Let all suspicions run deep
Into the clefts of endless nosiness and speculation.
If innuendos are unearthed,
Truth still cannot be buried alive.
Love is dangerous.

23

Cager on the court
Making high ferocious dunks
Smashing the backboard

24

Unafraid to fail
And willing to play life's games
No matter the score.

Childhood

When the street lights came on,
the impending darkness chased me home
And ran me smack dab into the front door.
White, old with hand-printed stains.
Dirt from playing & ink from printing.

There was no key
And no need to knock.
Just a whiff of Mama's fried chicken and collard
greens
Told me I was home.

We ate together before the Huxtables,
Just like the Evans and the Jeffersons.
Daddy was Fred Sanford and
Mama was Foxy Brown.

The street lights sounded the alarm:
Return home
To family
To safety

25

Back in the old days,
Neighbors had names we all knew.
Now we're all strangers.

26

Like running water
Words seep through open spaces
Not returning void

The Guilt of Regret

The piercing of my soul never ends
And the wounds seemingly never heal.
I can't get over what I've done.
Or didn't do.
  No one knows I am laden
    With yesterday's heavy load.
    Yesterday has gone and can't
  be undone,
    But still I languish at the
    thought of what might have been.
Did I waste too much time on purpose,
Or did time decide it would not wait?
    It moved as hastily as it
  came
    And left me bewildered in
  the wind.
When I was young, time seemed as if it would
last,
Yet age has found its fingers digging in the skin of
my youth.
Now
  I am
  Middle-aged.

Leave me to my guilt of regret and let the anguish
run its course.
Surely, I have tomorrow to make amends,
And forgive myself for what I've done.
Or left undone.

27

Time like a rogue thief,
Stealing, robbing, destroying.
Marauding bandit.

28

The changing of leaves
Rustles of trees on fall days,
The wind gives applause.

29

As the day goes by,
The sun poses for pictures.
Capture the moment.

30

My mind houses dreams.
Outside is reality.
What lies in between?

31

In a crowded room
With all kinds of sights and sounds,
Lonely hearts beat loud.

Home

Home sweet home.

In the comfort of my own.

There's only one voice I hear,

And it comes out of my mouth and into my ear.

32

From just dust of earth
Infused breath of God Himself.
I become hue man.

Surrender

I started writing you a poem.
I stopped.
How many more ways can I say I love you
Or
I want you?
It's perfectly clear
To the both of us:
One will win.
Someone will lose.
I give in...

33

The Spirit of God
Floods my mind with grateful thoughts
I'm overtaken.

34

Beautiful and bold,
Sister friends are like blue skies
And pristine beaches.

35

Where waters flow free
The trees grow along the way
They bend but don't break.

Ode to the Storied Franchise

Legends reign supreme in purple and gold
As this storied **L.A.** franchise never gets old.
Kings in the palace of the basketball court
Ever the beloved **venue** of any sport.
Rings acknowledge you above the rest.
Sixteen times you've been crowned the best.

36

Poetry loves me
Like no one else can move me;
Its warmth soothes me.

37

Life is fleeting wind
To grasp it and hold on tight
Is merely a wish.

Self-Possessed

You stand in front of the mirror— naked.

And I watch you.

I am drawn to your soft brown eyes.

I'd call you Asian.

The slant of your eyes captivate me.

I give you a wry smile.

I wonder who else I can mesmerize.

I kiss you. You kiss back. My same wry smile

Tests your sexiness.

I am that brown chocolate girl with freckles.

My hands rub together. I wonder—

Is it possible for all this loveliness to be contained?

My right hand rubs your left shoulder.

You brush your hand over your curly black hair.

And I see myself—

Again.

About the Author

Bummi Niyonu Anderson is a writer and author. She has written six books, including *I Like it When: A Collection of Love Poems*, *You are a Masterpiece: Seeing Yourself as God Sees You*, and *Gumbo Soul: Book of Poetry*."

She is also co-founder of *Renaissance Connection, Inc.* with her twin sister, Femi. Renaissance Connection is committed to educating others on the connection between art and life by sponsoring other artists/authors, art exhibitions, and teaching on fine art and writing.

For more than thirty years, she he has shared her poetry on college campuses, at churches, at cultural centers, and in poetry magazines and anthologies. An avid sports fan, Bummi has also written for Laker Nation, a fan blog for the Los Angeles Lakers.

Bummi has a Master's degree in English & Creative Writing. A graduate of Albany State University, she currently teaches English at her alma mater.

She resides in Albany, Georgia.

To order a copy of *Moods* or any other book or to read online writings by Bummi Niyonu Anderson, visit:

Website: www.bummianderson.com

TO CONTACT THE AUTHOR:

Facebook: Bummi Niyonu Anderson

Twitter: @BumminAnderson

Email: bummia@hotmail.com

www.ingramcontent.com/pod-product-compliance
Lightning Source LLC
Chambersburg PA
CBHW071154090426
42736CB00012B/2328